Threats against Russia's Information Society

Jan Softa

Preface

The interest in information security steadily increases among researchers in different disciplines. My interest in information security began in 2001 when I wrote a study about how the Y2K bug, also known as the millennium bug, ended up on the political agenda in Russia, Sweden, and the USA as a security problem. Since then, I have written different articles and reports on the subject, and much has happened in this field. More and more countries have taken the leap from being industrial societies to being information societies. Societies are becoming increasingly dependent upon information technology, and thereby it is important to reduce vulnerabilities in the information infrastructure and combat threats against such an information society. During the years it has become evident to me that this topic has gained more and more attention from politicians, the media, researchers, the private sector, and the public in general.

Moreover, it has to be mentioned that this book contains several Internet sources that no longer are available. Even though this book was written during a six to seven month period, I printed and collected material from Internet a couple of years before I began writing. Please do not let this decrease the validity of the conclusions I have made. It is not uncommon for Internet sources to disappear in this information age, often due to issues of funding. Still, I hope this book will be read with great interest.

ISBN: 1-4196-9204-6

Visit www.Booksurge.com to order additional copies

Table of contents

Threats against Russia's Information Society

1. Introduction

1.1. Background

Up until the end of the Cold War the political security agenda of the Soviet Union was dominated by threats from antagonistic states and NATO. In particular, the disintegration of the Soviet Union and the loss of the Eastern European States meant new conditions for the security landscape in Europe. A vacuum emerged within the security policy area, which at the time was considered a "window of opportunity" among the security establishment in Russia.[1] Questions that concerned security policy focus among politicians, militaries, and scholars no longer only spotlighted the arms race. This meant that different actors within the security establishment could put forward other questions as possible threats against society.[2] Economic security, information security, and ecological

---

[1] Kingdon, J. 1995.
[2] For an in-depth theoretical discussion about the security establishment see, Eriksson, J. 2001, p. 150-152; and for a detailed discussion about agenda-setting theory, see Kingdon, J. 1995 and Hinnfors, M. 1995.

security thereby became part of "the" agenda.[3] In this way, Russia, like most nations in the West, accepted a broader security agenda. Other questions, such as the population's increasingly failing health, were also framed as threats against society but were not given equal importance. During the latest ten-year period, Russia's ambition to become an information society has accelerated. In today's Russia, information technical solutions influence the way Russia does businesses and how Russia governs their state. The information age has created incredible possibilities concerning how societies disseminate, collect, and use information. The communication between people and the access to information has appreciably been facilitated through information technology (IT). However, technical development seldom means only advantages; it also means challenges.[4] During the last decades, the development of IT products and systems has been very rapid, and the use of IT has increased considerably. A common observation is it has made societies more vulnerable. Moreover, IT-related threats are often invisible. An actor can operate from anywhere in the world, making it difficult to identify a threat and its aim. Moreover, the number of persons with sufficient computer knowledge of how to disseminate computer viruses and with capacity to carry out attacks against the IT infrastructure is increasing.[5] Some researchers consider it plausible that this "silent revolution" will influence and change the international system and people's living conditions just as much as

---

[3] "The Foreign Policy Concept of the Russian Federation", p. 2.
[4] Softa, J. 2003; Leijonhielm, et. al., 2000.
[5] Softa, J. 2002.

the end of the Cold War.[6] Others are of the opinion that there has been a displacement from a world of enemies to a world of dangers and risks[7], and that the IT revolution, despite its advantages, has increased vulnerability in society due to dependency on complex, computerized systems.

1.2. Purpose

My purpose here is to examine which threats against its information society the Russian governmental power considers valid, if the threats have changed over time, and if this discussion of threats is a prioritised question in Russia. I also identify which authorities that currently are working with these issues or have in the past, and whether Russia is participating in international cooperations in order to combat threats against its information society. Finally, I examine how the Russian political elite view threats against its information society, and compares how that perception differs from to real, existing threats.

Threats against and vulnerabilities in information society have taken a salient role in the political security agenda in many states. One reason is that the IT infrastructure has a vital function in a modern society since other infrastructures, such as the power networks and telecommunications, have become increasingly dependent upon IT in order to function. The figure beneath illustrates dependencies among infrastructures.

---

[6] Alberts & Papp, 1997, p. xiv.
[7] Beck, 1999, p. 3.

Figure 1. Dependencies among infrastructures

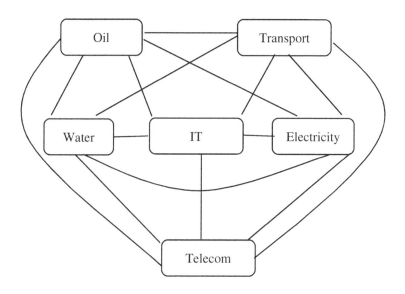

1.3. Material

In this book, I have used research papers, media, interviews, and public governmental documents. In particular, I have used documents ratified by the Russian Duma, such as Russia's information security doctrine and the Russian Federations concept for information security in communication networks.[8] In order to find out what opinions politicians and officials have on the subject, I have used media, books, and research reports, such as *The Russian Military Ability in a Ten-year Perspective* from the Swedish Defence Research Institute.[9]

---

[8] A security doctrine can be perceived as an overall declaration of what the Russian government wants to declare as threatening to their interests.
[9] Leijonhielm, et. al., 1999.

1.4. Preconditions for the book

In order to understand and explain the policy area of IT security, it is necessary to consider three aspects of security policies—threats, functions, and values to protect—together with protective measures.[10] In this study, the analysis is focused on the first aspect —threats—or rather the perception of threats, which is compared with concrete threats against information society.

A traditional approach begins with the notion that by analysing the world, we can decide what actually is threatening. But this disregards that different actors evaluate events and other phenomena in various ways. Some may consider a military invasion as a threat, while others perceive it as liberation. Framing something as a threat—much like framing something in positive terms—is essentially a normative action, i.e., a choice between different methods of evaluation. This study focuses on different actors' *perceptions* of threats, i.e., threat *images*.[11]

Furthermore, I present which threat images against Russia's information society are being considered, in particular which types of threats are most salient on the agenda. For example, are cyber attacks or construction flaws emphasized as the biggest threat?[12] Consequently, there can be several different threat images

---

[10] Eriksson, J. 2004, p. 118.
[11] Eriksson, J. 2001, p. 1-2.
[12] A more in-depth explanation on what types of threats exist is presented in the analytical framework.

against an information society that actors within the information security sector try to put on the political security agenda.

Primarily, this book focuses on the governmental level since a detailed description of the private sector, Medias' role, and different sub-national levels of society, such as the regional and municipal, would make the study too extensive and difficult to grasp.

In order to decrease vulnerabilities in an information society, it is important for the public sector to cooperate with the private sector, because they know which weaknesses exist and which improvements must be implemented in the business sector. IT companies have expert knowledge about vulnerabilities in their developed software. However, I have not found any written sources that discuss the need for special forums of private/public partnership. It would be necessary to conduct interviews with representatives from the Russian business community, which was not possible within the time frame for this study. But I am of the opinion that such a study would be a valuable piece of the puzzle in order to understand how it would be possible to cooperate in order to reduce threats against information society.

The Russian information security doctrine is an important document in regards to understanding how information security has been framed in Russia. This doctrine contains Russia's perception of what is included in the concept of information security. However, in this study not all of these aspects are discussed; rather, the focus is on which threat images, e.g., attacks and disturbances, exist according to the Russian governmental power. Citizens' constitutional freedoms and rights within the information area are not considered, nor do I investigate how a deteriorated level in the education system within the computer information area can become a problem.[13]

Although there are no established universal perceptions about differences between information security and IT threats, it is possible to make a distinction between them. Threats against (and vulnerabilities in) IT concern its infrastructure, hardware, and software, such as application programmes. Information security includes all this as well as the need for protections against disinformation and propaganda operations with communication technology and newspapers, etc.

In the Russian information security doctrine, protections against unknown actors' propaganda are discussed. These actors can use computers, printed media, radio, and television both within and outside Russia's borders. However, my aim in this book is not to examine all these channels because unknown actors' propaganda does not affect the function of the IT infrastructure.

Rather, the study focuses on how threats against IT can develop into crises in Russian society, which means that the focus is not on the offensive aspects of how Russia can use IT, but on the defensive.[14] In other words, my focus is not on how Russian

---

[13] "Doktrina informacionnoj bezapasnosti Rossiskoj Federacii". p. 5-6, 8.
[14] For a comprehensive explanation of offensive and defensive aspects see, Alberts, D. S. 1996; Denning, D., 1999.

hackers can be a threat against the surrounding world but on threats against Russia's information society.

2. Analytical framework

Theories about how problems are framed can be used in order to study how certain threats against an information society have ended up on the political agenda. After a brief description of these theories, I discuss possible threats against an information society, actor threats as well as non-actor. Finally, the subjective perception of threats against an information society is compared with concrete IT threats.

Political problems and interests must be comprehended and presented convincingly before they can end up on the political agenda. How political questions are legitimately framed and related to each other decides the direction of the political process. Researchers Schön and Rein define framing as a way to choose, organize, interpret, and make a complex reality understandable in order to achieve guidance for knowledge, analysis, persuasion, and action.[15] In other words, framing can be considered an attitude to a problematic situation (for example the possible consequences on society of a hacker attack) that makes it possible to act.[16]

Entman states that:

---

[15] Rein, M. & Schön, D. 1993, p. 146.
[16] Mörth, U. 1999, p. 1.

"Frames define problems—determine what a causal agent is doing with what costs and benefits, usually measured in terms of common cultural values; diagnose causes—identify the forces creating problems; make moral judgments—evaluate causal agents and their effects; and suggest remedies—offer and justify treatments for the problems and predict their likely effects".[17]

In this book I use three of these four criteria. To *define the problem*, I investigate which threats and vulnerabilities the Russian governmental power frames against its information society. To *diagnose the causes*, I identify the threats that cause problems. And to *suggest remedies*, I investigate if the Russian governmental power has introduced regulations, drafted working papers, and founded, developed, and reconstructed organisations, etc.

In order for threats to receive a lot of attention, important actors, such as politicians, officials, experts, media, lobby groups, and academics, must frame them.[18] This study focuses on politicians' and officials' perception of threats, but also which threats are emphasized in policy documents.

The concrete/real threats that can cause crises in an information society are divided in two main types: *actor threats* and *non-actor threats*. *Actor threats* are digital and physical; an example of a digital threat would be a cyber attack targeted against homepages, e-mail, IP-addresses, and so on. These attacks can be

---

[17] Entman, R. 1993.
[18] This is equivalent to the meaning of the Copenhagen school *"securitizing actors"* and to the concept "policy entrepreneurs" in agenda-setting theory. See, Buzan, Wæver and de Wilde, 1998, p. 40-42; Kingdon, J., 1995.

carried out by actors, such as young hackers and crackers[19] motivated by curiosity, but also by more threatening actors such as criminals, spies, terrorists, and rogue states. Motives can be to steal, manipulate, and destroy data in order to influence decision-making processes or to get access to information in companies and authorities. A physical threat, on the other hand, is an intentional or unintentional external impact on the infrastructure. Unintentional threats can be caused by poor security routines that increase incidents or the human factor causing accidents.[20] An intentional threat can be someone with a sledgehammer or an electromagnetic weapon[21] that sabotages computers or the infrastructure.

---

[19] CRACKER: an individual who attempts to access computer systems without authorization. Crackers are often malicious, as opposed to hackers, and have many means at their disposal for breaking into systems. HACKER: a person who delights in having an intimate understanding of the internal workings of a system —computers and computer networks in particular. The term is almost universally misused in a pejorative context, where cracker would be the term. Although *cracker* is the correct term for malicious actions directed against computer systems, the term *hacker* is becoming synonymous through popular usage. See links at Space and Electronic Warfare Lexicon: http://www.sew-lexicon.com/gloss_c.htm#CRACKER and http://www.sew-lexicon.com/gloss_h.htm

[20] SEMA: 0753/2003, 2003.

[21] Electromagnetic weapons are also known as HPM-weapons—High Powered Microwave Weapons. Some of the problems HPM-weapons can cause are presented in a paper by Softa, J. 2003, p. 10, and in an overhead presentation by Wiik, M. 2003. It is explained that an HPM-weapon can disrupt or knock out electric instruments and systems. HPM-weapons affect technical infrastructures such as power networks, the Internet, and banking systems, but also medical equipment, electronic door looks and so on. HPM-weapons are used primarily because most civilian electronic equipment does not have a sufficient level of protection against these weapons, and few physical barriers restrict the effect of the weapon. For instance, it works through house walls. The consequences can be that life and health are affected, that economic activity is disrupted and that computer programs are destroyed. Also, the knowledge of these weapons and their components is spreading around the globe.

Figure 2. Matrix of threats against the function of an information society.[22]

	IT-based threats	Non IT-based threats
Actor threats	Digital	Physical
Non-actor threats	Construction flaws	Natural disasters

Source: Softa, 2003 and Malm, Softa, Andersson & Lindström, 2003.

Non-actor threats are construction flaws and natural disasters. Construction flaws arise when systems have insufficient security levels or when they malfunction (in the case of computer bugs). Natural disasters that are a threat against the IT infrastructure include blizzards, earthquakes, volcanic eruptions, and avalanches. These can cause interruptions in the power supply and the telecommunication, which are a precondition for the function of the Internet, e-mail, etc.

What is considered threatening and end-up on the political agenda are not necessarily the most urgent threats.[23] Moreover, a threat can be perceived to have increased even if in reality it has not been changed from one time to another. Norris et al give examples of this when they point out that what drastically

---

[22] Those who want to study how different actors with digital means and by causing physical damage can disrupt the function of IT can benefit from using the matrix presented by Nicander, L. and Ranstorp, M., 2004. In the matrix above, these are represented by the actor-based digital and physical threats. In this book I am also studying how non-actor threats such as construction flaws and natural disasters can be a threat against an information society.
[23] Eriksson, J. 2004.

changed in USA after September 11 was the American *perception* of threats from world terrorism, not the actual *reality*.[24] In this same vein, Jervis notes that it is worthwhile to study decision-making in order to find out if differences exist between perception and the reality. He is of the opinion that specialists in neither psychology nor international relations have studied how decision-makers draw their conclusions on the basis of information. It has been assumed that decision-makers most often consider the world as quite accurate and that misunderstandings can be seen as temporary. According to Jervis, this assumption is incorrect.[25] If the subjective framing of threats is compared with concrete threats against information society, we start to see a different picture. Based on this, I ask, has the Russian governmental power, like many other states, emphasized a certain type of threat against its information society?[26]

---

[24] Norris, P., Montague, K., & M. Just, 2003.

[25] Jervis, R., 1976, p. 3.

[26] Estonia is a state that emphasized digital threats against its information society more than other types of threats. See, Softa, J., 2004, p. 363. In Iceland, natural disasters have been emphasized as the largest threat against the function of their information society. See, Holmgren, J. and Softa, J., 2003.

3. Threats against Russia's Information Society

The end of the Cold War caused a vacuum in the political security landscape that made it possible for other threats to get accepted on the political security agenda in Russia. It changed from a narrow focus on antagonistic states and NATO to include terrorism, international organized crime, and threats against Russia's information society.

It is evident that the Russian state has aspirations of becoming a leading information society. With *The Strategy for Developing an Information Society in Russia*, the Russian government has developed a strategy to achieve this with control parameters that should be reached by 2015. Russia can be placed among the twenty leading countries of the world in international ratings in the field of progress of an information society, while on a national level Russia is rated in the top ten for penetration of IT, meaning that 100 percent of the population has access to information and communication technologies and that no less than 75 percent of house facilities have access to personal computers connected to the Internet.[27]

However, Russia is far from its target of becoming a leading information society. In the Networked Readiness Index (NRI) 2006-2007, which defines a nation's or a society's ability to

---

[27] "Strategiya razvitiya informacionnogo obshhestva v Rossi".

21

take advantage of the latest development in information and communication technology,[28] Russia is rated at 70 of 122 examined states, between the Philippines at 69 and Azerbaijan at 71. Among the highest rated, Denmark is number one, Sweden is number two, USA is number seven, and Germany is 16. Although Russia has not integrated IT to the same extent as the U.S. and Sweden, the Russian governmental power has noticed how vulnerabilities in IT can be a threat against Russia's interests and how they can generate deficiencies in critical infrastructure.[29]

At a United Nation (UN) meeting in the year 2000, the Russian representative Anatonov said that:

"The information revolution is a global phenomenon that influences all aspects in society, such as international attitudes, the policy, the economy, the financial sector, science and culture. Information resources have become one of the most valuable national and international assets. At the same time there is a deep concern about the potential threats this progress can have on the international peace, stability and security. Therefore, it is important to limit potential international confrontations within the IT sphere".[30]

---

[28] "The Network Readiness Index 2006-2007 rankings".

[29] Critical infrastructure is infrastructure that is vital for the functioning of a society. It might mean nuclear plants, power supply, telecommunications, or hospitals. In this study critical infrastructure concerns power supply, information technology infrastructure and telecommunication networks.

[30] A. I. Anatonov was Russia's representative at an UN meeting the 19th of October 2000 that discussed international security within the information and telecommunication areas. See, "Vystuplenie predstavitelya Rossii A.I. Anatonova v Pervom Komitete 55-j sessii GA OON pri predstavlenii proekta rezolyucii"Dostizheniya v sfere informatizacii i telekommunikacii v kontekste mezhdunarodnoj bezopasnosti" 19 oktyabrya 2000 goda".

3.1. The Change of the IT Threat Image

The development of information technology began later in the former Soviet Union than in the West, in the beginning because of a passive or even negative attitude towards this technology and later on because of prevailing restrictions in technology export from the West to the East.[31] These restrictions subsided when the glasnost-period emerged, which led to a rapid development of technology in the early 90s, especially in Russia.[32] But technical development rarely comes with only advantages, but also with problems.

An understanding of this problem when it concerns IT has long existed with the Russian government. In 1992 information security was already being discussed at the then newly established Russian Security Council.[33] The year after that, the Federal Agency for Government Communications and Information (FAPSI) was established by a decree from the president. Until 2003, FAPSI were one of the main governmental actors that worked with detecting threats against Russia's information society.[34] The establishment of FAPSI indicated two important aspects. Firstly, early on it was understood that the information technology would cause new threats against society and that solutions were required. Secondly, it suggested that Russian

---

[31] The restriction was called Coordinating Committee for Multilateral Export Controls (COCOM).
[32] Leijonhielm, et. al., 1999, p. 247.
[33] Leijonhielm, et. al., 2000, p. 247.
[34] "FAPSI Operations"; "Federal Agency for Government Communications and Information".

authorities were working with these subjects far earlier than threats against Russia's information society were formulated into an information security *doctrine.*

In the late nineties a handful of *laws* defined the primary concepts of information policy in Russia. An example of this is the federal law "On Information, Informatization and the Defence on Information," which addresses government responsibilities for information provision. It indicates that the government is obligated to develop and protect information resources as well as to establish conditions for their distribution. Regarding information technology, the government is charged with the task of developing policies that reflect the "contemporary world development of information technologies."[35] This *law* and others indicate that during the nineties information security gained more and more attention in Russia.

However, it was not until 1997 that the importance of the country's information security was mentioned in a security *concept.*[36] In this concept a variety of different threats were discussed, such as international terrorism, smuggling of drugs, environmental problems, diffusion of weapons of mass destruction,

---

[35] Other examples are the constitution and the presidential decree "On the Concepts of National Security of the Russian Federation," which provide basic guidance on this issue. The following laws: "On Security," "On Government Secrets," "On Participation in International Information Exchanges," "On Proper Security of Programs for Computers and Databases," and "On Copyright and Interfacing Laws" formed the core of legislative efforts in information policy. See, "Information Technology and Legislation in Russia".
[36] Leijonhielm, et. al, 2000, p. 247.

and deficiency of information security.[37] However, nothing suggested that threats against information security should gain higher priority than the other. Also in Russia's national security concepts from January 19, 2000, the same threats were identified. But neither in this document was information security stronger prioritised. Nevertheless, the threat image against an information society has become more developed. In the national security concept from 2000 it was emphasized that:

"There are growing threats to the national security of the Russian Federation in the information sphere. There is a major threat in the striving of some countries to dominate the world information space and oust Russia from the foreign and domestic information market; the elaboration by some countries of a concept of information wars, which provides for the creation of means of dangerous influence on the information spheres of other world countries; the disruption of the normal operation of the information and telecommunication systems and of the safety of the information resources, as well as attempts to gain unwarranted access to them".[38]

The public pallet of threat images became more extensive and specific with Putin's ratification of the information security doctrine on September 9, 2000.[39] It also meant that now threats

---

[37] "National Security Concept of the Russian Federation—1997", p. 1-2. For more examples, see same document, p. 11.

[38] "National Security Concept of the Russian Federation—2000", p. 5.

[39] It is difficult to get a clear picture of what actors that have been involved in the drawing up of the doctrine. But it is clear that a sub-committee for information security at the Russian Duma was leading in this work. However, this sub-committee does not exist anymore. Another actor is the interdepartmental department for information security in the Russian Security Council and maybe also FAPSI and Department K. Persons that have been involved are Tsygichko and Chereskin, who work at ISA. See, Chereskin, D. and Tsygichko, V., 2005; Porfiriev, B. et al, 2005.

against Russian information society were high on the political security agenda. The doctrine described Russia's perception on information security and became the foundation for the government policy. Security was now to be achieved by preparing proposals for the improvement of laws, methods, research technology, and organisation in Russia. In the information security doctrine, information was considered an important part of today's society and assumed to have a strong influence on Russia's political, economic, and military security. Since the use of the information technology in Russia was determined to increase, society would gradually become more dependent on securing information in IT for the national security.[40]

When the Security Council made public the information security doctrine, acting President Putin (1999-2008) emphasized the information technology's importance in the new millennium: "It is obvious that the morrow of the world politics and world economy will be determined by information resources." Putin also considered that "the future of our country also depends on the solutions of the problems in the [information] sphere."[41]

An even stronger focus on developing Russia as an information society was founded in 2002, when the federal programme Elektronnaya Rossiya went into force.[42] In March 2002, Andrey Korotkov was appointed as first executive minister of the Ministry for Communication and Information with the task

---

[40] "Doktrina informacionnoj bezapasnosti Rossiskoj Federacii", p. 1.
[41] "Russia Approves Draft Information Security Doctrine".
[42] "e-russia"; "Resursnoe obespechenie programmy".

of running the directorate for *e-russia*. The directorate is a body responsible for the implementation of Russia's e-program[43]; their main purpose is to rapidly increase e-commerce and the use of Internet in the country. Russia intends to invest 76-150 millions roubles from 2002 to 2010.[44]

Moscow also has its own e-program that was set to be implemented between 2002 and 2007. When Moscow launched its own program, e-Moscow, it broke a financial record for the city, presenting a five-year development plan worth two billion USD.[45] The Institute of the Information Society Russia produced an "Information Society Moscow Concept." It was decided they needed not only the concept but also needed the action plans and programs. Yuri Hohlov, chairman of the board of the Institute of the Information Society, talked about the beginnings of the e-Moscow program, saying that initially there had been no strategy as to how to promote e-development for the city.

> "There were a lot of different projects and activities running in Moscow, but they were all separate entities. We started to build a strategy of how to move toward the Information Society, and how to convert the industrial potential to the Information Society potential".[46]

In the *Concept for Information Security in Russia's Communication Networks*, which made public in 2003, it became more evident what was considered threatening; the

---

[43] "U.S. & FCS E-Russia Program—Update August 2002".
[44] "e-russia"; "Resursnoe obespechenie programmy".
[45] "E-Moscow—a $2 Billion Program".
[46] "E-Moscow—a $2 Billion Program".

document pointed out that an insufficient protection of communication networks made Russia vulnerable for hostile attacks and provocative campaigns from criminals. Moreover, the information and telecommunication networks had become increasingly interconnected, which means that the Russian networks became more dependent on the security in other States' networks.[47]

The Strategy for Developing an Information Society in Russia, 2007, was prepared in accordance with Russia's international obligations and the information security doctrine and federal laws. In this document, an insufficient protection of communication networks in both the public and private sector is framed as a problem. Also, the spreading of terrorist and extremist ideology and propagation of violence on Internet is, as expected, framed as a threat. In order to combat this, Russian law enforcement bodies are instructed to interact with their counterparts in foreign states. Furthermore, in order to decrease vulnerabilities in Russia's information society, it is deemed important that Russia participate in the development of the international standards that concern information security and harmonize national standards with international.[48]

Nowadays, threats against Russia's information society are an accepted threat image among the political elite. In 2007, acting Foreign Minister Sergey Lavrov told the Russian

---

[47] "Kontseptciya informacionnoj bezopasnosti setej svyazi obshhego pol`zovaniya vzaimouvyazannoj setej svyazi Rossiskoj Federacii", p. 8-9.
[48] "Strategiya razvitiya informacionnogo obshhestva v Rossi".

Duma that the Ministry of Foreign Affairs was considering measures to coordinate Internet controls to counter cyber-terrorism. He accused terrorists of using information technologies for communication, recruiting, training, and propaganda.[49]

An important conclusion is that early on in Russia there was an understanding that new technology causes new vulnerabilities and threats. But, as in other countries, there was no comprehensive knowledge about which threats and vulnerabilities were being faced. Through the years, one has undergone a process where threats against Russia's information society have become increasingly specified and extensive, thus the implementation of laws on IT-security, national action plans, and the assignment of "information security tasks" to Russia's intelligence organizations. Another important conclusion is that Russian authorities worked with threats against information society before these questions were formulated in an information security doctrine. This suggests that the framing of IT threat images has a bottom-up perspective. Officials have had an opportunity to frame what IT threats that will be salient in different security concepts and the information security doctrine.

3.2. Priority on the agenda

That threats against the information society have high priority on the Russian agenda becomes evident in different statements of the security establishment and of policy documents. Several reasons

---

[49] "Citing Cyber-Terrorism Threat, Russia Explores Internet Controls".

are mentioned as to why these threats should be a prioritised subject on the political security agenda.

Within the Russian security establishment there are those who consider that, next to nuclear war, cyber warfare is the most serious threat to any society, and who consider cyber warfare to be just like any other type of warfare. They believe that Russia should have the right to defend itself with conventional weapons as well as weapons of mass destruction.[50] At a conference 1995 more than one military officer was of the opinion that:

> "[f]rom a military point of view, the use of Information Warfare against Russia or its armed forces will categorically not be considered a non-military phase of a conflict whether there were causalities or not ... considering the possible catastrophic use of strategic information warfare means by an enemy, whether on economic or state command and control systems, or on the combat potential of the armed forces ... Russia retains the right to use nuclear weapons first against the means and forces and information warfare, and then against the aggressor state itself".[51]

Tsygichko, who was involved in the work with writing a draft of the information security doctrine to which he and among others Chereskin contributed their knowledge about information security, is of the opinion that the development of a global information society has led to a modern society slowly becoming entirely dependent on the information infrastructure. Russia's dependence on this infrastructure makes society relatively vulnerable for attacks from hostile states, terrorists, criminal groups, and individual

---

[50] Hildreth, S. 2001, p. 10 and 11.
[51] Tsymbal, V. I. 1995, p. 17.

saboteurs. Therefore, it is of greatest importance to national security that the information sphere has a high priority at the governmental power.[52]

Chereskin and Tsygichko point out that IT is used in many parts of society and therefore must be protected. A major concern is that Internet is an open system, which makes it sensitive to hacker attacks and dissemination of viruses. Therefore, they are of the opinion that Russia must formulate a governmental policy for information security. Moreover, they believe that the information security doctrine is not in an optimal way explaining how the governmental power should carry out their information security work, even though it is positive that the doctrine was adopted because threats against Russia's information society got more attention.[53]

A central actor in framing threats against Russia is the Russian Security Council (henceforth called the Security Council). The Security Council drafts proposals to the Russian president

---

[52] Tsygichko, V., 2002, p. 27-28. Tsygichko and Chereskin are both professors and work at the Institute for System Analysis (ISA), located in Moscow. They and ISA research, among other things, information security. They have not only affected the drafting of the information security doctrine but have also been authors of other publications regarding information security, such as Polikanov, *Information Challenges to National and International Security, 2001;* Smoljan, *Internet v Rossii—Perspektivi Razvitiya [Internet in Russia – Perspective on the development], 2004;* Chereskin, *Problemi Upravleniya Informatsionnoj Bezopasnostyu, [Problem in the Management of Information Security], 2002;* Tsygichko, *Informacionnoe Oruzhie i Mezhdunarodnaya Informacinnaya Bezopasnost, [Information Weapons and the International Information Security], 2001*
[53] Chereskin, D. and Tsygichko, V., 2005.

31

concerning internal and external threats targeted against Russian citizens, their society, and their state.[54]

An interview from 2001 with Sherstyuka, the first executive secretary in the Russian Security Council, reveals that threats against its information society have a high priority with the Russian governmental power. Sherstyuka was of the opinion that since the information revolution influences economic development and society, information security will have an increasingly dominant place in government policy. The problem is considered to be that the dissemination of foreign information technology covers all social sectors and that it is common to use open information and communication systems, increasing threats from information weapon targeted against Russia's information infrastructure.[55]

The Security Council's concern for information security also became evident in November 2006, when the deputy secretary of the Russian Security Council, Valentin Sobolev, warned about potential terrorist attempts to use the Internet to penetrate the networks of the world's civilian and military nuclear sites and conduct acts of nuclear terrorism.[56]

---

[54] "Sovet bezopasnosti Rossijskoj federatsii – istoriya sozdaniya, pravovoj status, struktura i osnove napravleniya deyatel`nosti", p. 3. The Security Council consists of permanent members and other members appointed by the Russian president. In general, the permanent members are the minister of defence, the minister of foreign affairs and the Head of FSB. Other members can be executives in federal ministries and departments.
[55] "Interv`yu Pervogo Zamestitelya Sekretarya Soveta bezopasnosti Rossiskoj Federatcii V.P. Sherstyuka gazete "Krasnaya Zvezda", Opublikovannoe 24 Yanvarya 2001 goda", p. 3.
[56] "Citing Cyber-Terrorism Threat, Russia Explores Internet Controls".

In order to study which threat images have dominated Russia's agenda, we can also examine which interdepartmental commissions have been founded in the Security Council. These commissions have mainly similar duties but are responsible for different political areas. The duties consist in detecting possible threats and locating problems within their respective political areas, as well as preparing proposals in order to find suitable countermeasures and to implement these. Currently, there are seven different commissions, of which one works with information security.[57]

The interdepartmental commission for information security evaluates changes that can improve Russia's information security. One of its most important tasks is to find sources to evaluate external and internal information security threats.[58] The existence of a special commission for information security indicates that information security is prioritised in Russia.

It is also possible to see what threats that are considered to be the most urgent by examining whether the Duma and the president have ratified security concepts and doctrines that contain security policy such as Russia's national security concepts, Russia's military doctrine, maritime doctrine, ecology doctrine, and

---

[57] These are 1) the interdepartmental commission (TIC) for ecological security, 2) TIC for information security, 3) TIC for security in the economic and social sphere, 4) TIC for the citizens' security 5) TIC for military security, 6) TIC for problems within CIS, and 7) TIC for problems within strategic planning. See, "Mezhvedomstvennyè komissii soveta bezapasnosti Rossiskoj Federacii".
[58] "Mezhvedomstvennyè komissii soveta bezapasnosti Rossiskoj Federacii", p. 1-3.

information security doctrine.[59] The latter doctrine points out various threats against and vulnerabilities in Russia's information society. In 2003, the Russian Ministry for Communication and Information adopted the Concept for Information Security in Russia's Communication Networks, which in some aspects are a development of the information security doctrine. In this concept, the problem areas are more specified and can be perceived as an action plan in order to solve some of the threats mentioned in the information security doctrine.[60] The Strategy for Developing an Information Society has the objective to transform Russia into one of the world's leaders in post-industrial development and significantly bolster its information security. It also addresses many of the threats mentioned in the information security doctrine.[61]

There is clear evidence that threats against the Russian information society are a prioritised subject on the political security agenda in Russia. The aforementioned documents are proof of this, as well as the existence of the interdepartmental commission for information security in the Security Council and several other authorities that work with information security.

---

[59] "Kontseptciya naciona`lnoj bezopasnosti Rossiskoj Federacii"; "Voennaya doktrina Rossiskoj Federacii"; "E´kologicheskaya doktrina Rossiskoj Federacii"; "Morskaya doktrina Rossiskoj Federacii na period do 2020 goda"; "Doktrina informacionnoj bezapasnosti Rossiskoj Federacii".
[60] "Kontseptciya informacionnoj bezopasnosti setej svyazi obshhego pol`zovaniya vzaimouvyazannoj setej svyazi Rossiskoj Federacii", p. 8.
[61] "INTERNET LAW - Strategy for Developing an Information Society in Russia".

3.3. Responsible ministries, authorities and organisational changes

Since the dependency on IT in Russia is steadily increasing, it has also become more important for the governmental power to secure the function of this infrastructure. As mentioned before, Russian governmental bodies have been imposed to work with this task. At the Security Council the interdepartmental commission for information security became active in 1997.[62] The commission's task is to prepare proposals that the Security Council will discuss and take position to. One of the main tasks of the commission is to evaluate deficiencies in the information security. The Security Council functions as an advisory body to Russia's president.[63]

Also, the Duma's Committee on Information Security and ministries are responsible for ensuring a high level of information security in Russia. The Ministry of the Interior took responsibility for Department R and is now responsible for its successor Department K, which is combating cyber-criminals. Also EMERCOM, who work with civil defence management, are involved in the work of protecting and rebuilding the IT-infrastructure after natural disasters. The Ministry of Defence is responsible for the Directorate of Radio-Electronic Warfare. Finally, the Ministry of Communication and Information is responsible for developing and implementing action plans that

---

[62] "Mezhvedomstvennyè komissii soveta bezapasnosti Rossiskoj Federacii".
[63] "Mezhvedomstvennyè komissii soveta bezapasnosti Rossiskoj Federacii", p. 1-3.

ensure Russia's IT infrastructure becomes less vulnerable to threats.

During 1994 FAPSI replaced the Administration of Information Resources (AIR) that had been founded by the former KGB (in English, the Committee for State Security).[64] FAPSI was the Federal Agency for Government Communications and Information and held the main responsibility for Russia's information security.[65] The authority was imposed to control domestic crime, hackers, foreign intelligence services, and information weapons that could threaten Russia's security. In the middle of the 1990s, FAPSI came to play an even more important role. All public and cryptic communication traffic in Russia, both business and private, began to be monitored, and the domestic political development was followed by monitoring different opinions in Russia. Afterwards, this information was presented for the country's intelligence services. FAPSI was also the state's renter of signal communication to banks and other branches of the industry, and issued export and import licences to IT companies.[66]

---

[64] "Federal Agency for Government Communications and Information".

[65] FAPSI was created from the 8th (Government Communications) and 16th (Electronic Intelligence) Chief Directorates of the KGB. It is the equivalent of the American National Security Agency. According to the press, the structure of FAPSI copied the structure of the US National Security Agency, it included: chief R&D directorate, chief directorate of government communications, chief directorate of security of communications, chief directorate of information technology, special troops of FAPSI, Academy of Cryptography, Military School of FAPSI in Voronezh, sometimes referred as the world largest hacker's school, Military School of Communications in Orel, Moscow Department of Penza Scientific Research Electrotechnics Institute (МО ПНИЭИ), manufacturer of software and hardware used by the above agencies. See, "FAPSI".

[66] Saarelainen, J. p. 22-24.

After a presidential decree in March 2003, a number of governmental agencies merged or disappeared concurrently as new ones were established. The big winner of the reorganisation was the Federal Security Service (FSB) that both inherited parts of FAPSI and the whole the Federal Border Service (FPS), which included the border troops. FPS and FAPSI were abolished entirely.[67] FAPSI was divided between FSB, FSO (in English Federal Protection Service), and SVR (in English Foreign Intelligence Service).[68] There were several reasons for this, one of which being to streamline security structures. Furthermore, during the latter part of the 1990s, FAPSI was surrounded by rumours about corruption, which probably was a reason for its dismantling. At FSO the service for special communications and information was created. Most probably, this service was responsible for the signal protection with state authorities, while signal surveillance ended up at FSB's and SVR's direction.[69]

Since FAPSI was terminated, FSO has increased in importance within the information and communication areas, the task being to examine the communication in information networks and to acquire classified information. However, the main task was to work on defensive Information Operations and to provide safe

---

[67] "Normativnyè akty reglamentiruyushhie deyatel`nost fsb, Uprazdneny` FSNP i FAPSI, FPS peredana v FSB"; "Reforma specsluzhb nachalas. Tolko sovsem he tak, kak govoril Putin".

[68] Putin makes sweeping changes to power structures; Russian and Baltic Economies—the Week in Review 11 # 2003. FSO = *Federalnaya Sluzhba Okhrany* and SVR = *Sluzhba Vneshney Razvedki*.

[69] E-post: Carolina Vendil Pallin, FOI; "FSB Looks An Awful Lot Like The KGB"; "Special Communications and Information Service".

communication equipment in order to develop methods so as to preserve the information security in Russia and to protect information that contained government secrets.[70]

SVR is another of Russia's intelligence services that works with refuting external threats. It is very probable that SVR is aimed at gathering intelligence on economic and technical issues.[71] It works in cooperation with the Russian military intelligence organization GRU. A new "Law on Foreign Intelligence Organs" was passed by the State Duma and the Federation Council in late 1995 and signed into effect by then-President Boris Yeltsin on 10 January 1996. The law authorized the SVR's Directorate I to conduct electronic surveillance in foreign countries. This directorate analyzes and distributes intelligence data and publishes a daily current events summary for the president.[72]

GRU (*Glavnoje Razvedyvatel'noje Upravlenije*), meaning Main Intelligence Directorate, operates SIGINT, which is an intelligence gathering agency that uses interception of signals, whether between people (i.e., COMINT or communications intelligence) or between machines (i.e., ELINT or electronic intelligence), or mixtures of the two. As sensitive information is often encrypted, SIGINT often involves the use of cryptanalysis.[73]

Today FSB (in English, the Federal Security Service) is one of the most powerful Russian governmental authorities. For

---

[70] "Sluzhba spetsial`noj svyazi i informacii federal`noj sluzhby oxrany` Rossijskoj Federacii".
[71] "Sluzhba vneschnej razvedki Rossii".
[72] "Foreign Intelligence Service (Russia)".
[73] "GRU"; "SIGINT".

the Russian governmental power, FSB constitutes an important operational tool in the struggle against terrorism, espionage, and all kind of crime. The FSB has mandates to carry out Information Operations. As an example the SORM-project[74] used technology that made it possible to monitor all telephone and Internet traffic.[75]

SORM (in English System of Ensuring Investigative Activity) was introduced 1995 when the State gave FSB legal permission to monitor all telecommunication. When its next generation, SORM 2, was ready to be implemented in 1998, a new regulation gave FSB permission to monitor the Internet. Now each Internet operator was legally obligated to install equipment on its servers where every credit card transaction, e-mail message, or homepage clicks could be checked without the monitored person knowing it. Then the information was sent directly to FSB[76], allowing them to monitor the Russian citizens' Internet traffic. A senior FSB official, Dmitri Frolov, also proposed mandatory registration of all mobile phones with Internet capabilities.[77] However, the official reason with the SORM-project was to support the fight against crime in Russia. To add insult to injury, Internet providers were to pay for the equipment; and despite the original noisy resistance of Internet providers, they complied.[78]

---

[74] SORM is an abbreviation of Sistema Operativno-Rozysknykh Meropriyatii.
[75] "Federal`naya sluzhba bezopasnosti Rossii (FSB)"; "Otchet FSB za 2003 god".
[76] "SORM—Russia´s big brother"; "Russia—Surveillance of Communications".
[77] "Citing Cyber-Terrorism Threat, Russia Explores Internet Controls".
[78] Moreover, the initial law providing legislative support for SORM is the "Law on Operational-Search Activities in the Russian Federation" The law was put in place on March 13, 1992. The law established the legal framework for the system. The initial announcement of its implementation was outlined in a Ministry of Communication decree that was first published in 1992 and amended

During 1983, Department R was established in the Soviet Ministry of the Interior and shortly after achieved the status as an intelligence service. The department functioned as the Ministry of Interior's technical security service and was imposed to protect computer and telecommunication systems against external intrusions. Due to changes in a 1998 legislation, Department R was deprived its status as an intelligence service and was incorporated in the judicial system's authorities. Then, in the year 2000, the department for control of cyber crime (Department K) was established at the Russian Ministry of Interior.[79] They are informally called Russia's cyber police. Department K has three main tasks; the first includes hacking of computer systems, theft of login codes, money and dissemination of computer viruses. The second main task is to counteract "telecommunications crime," such as using an illegal access to telecommunication network when establishing a telecommunication centre.[80] The third main task is to counteract illegal use of technical hardware that been designed to illegally monitor and disclose secrets in people's private lives.[81]

A part of the IT security work is prospective. A way is to use IT security standards in order to increase the general level of information security in society. Russia's Bureau for

in 1995. The decree "On the Use Means of Communication to Facilitate Investigative Activities of the Ministry of Security of the Russian Federation." See, "Information Technology and Legislation in Russia".

[79] "Chief of "K" department is interviewed on cyber-crimes".

[80] Background to the problems with telecenters. In Russia it was not uncommon that instead of using a home phone people went to telecenters that offered a much lower calling rate than regular phone operators. The problem seemed to be that the telecenters could have an illegal connection to communication networks.

[81] "Chief of "K" department is interviewed on cyber-crimes".

Standardisation is entitled the Federal Agency for Technical Regulation and Metrology, which is referred to as *Rostexregulirovanii*. In this organisation, there are different committees. The work with IT standardisations is in committee 22, which also is referred to as the technical committee for information technology. Askold Pjavchenko is executive director in this committee, which is Russia's representative in the International Standardization Organization (ISO) that also works with developing international IT security standards.[82] It is costly and non-functional to develop national IT standards, and therefore the committee discusses which international security standards are appropriate to implement in Russia's society. The objective is to notice problems and to provide IT standards that reduce possible vulnerabilities in the management of IT and its infrastructure.[83] Thereby, the general IT security level is increased in Russia's society.

A somewhat unexpected actor in this context is EMERCOM, the Ministry for extraordinary events. The ministry has various departments, commissions and boards, whose main task is to work with different civil defence issues. Of interest in this study is the Department for Disaster Management, the Commission for Control of Forest Fires and the Commission for Flooding, the personnel of which are engaged in large natural disasters, as

---

[82] "TK No022"; "Rostexregulirovanii bydet uchastovat` v vy`borax v Sovet ISO"; "Kontseptciya informacionnoj bezopasnosti setej svyazi obshhego pol`zovaniya vzaimouvyazannoj setej svyazi Rossiskoj Federacii", p. 17 and 25.
[83] "TK No022"; "Rostexregulirovanii bydet uchastovat` v vy`borax v Sovet ISO".

flooding and earthquakes, which can cause interruptions in IT infrastructure, power networks, and telecommunication networks.[84]

The most important finding is the existence of many different State bodies, ministries and authorities that are working with counteracting various threats against Russia's information society. Some have an advisory role, like the Interdepartmental Commission for Information Security, while FSO works operationally with signal intelligence and Department K tries to disclose cyber criminals. The Russian Bureau for Standardisations IT security work is prospective.

---

[84] "Ministry of Extraordinary Situations"; "Zadatji Ministersva".

Figure 3. Scheme of ministries, agencies, and intelligence services that work with managing threats against Russia's information society[85]

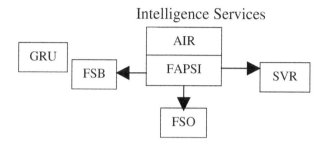

---

[85] AIR, FAPSI and Department R have ceased to exist.

3.4. International cooperation

As described above, there are several Russian authorities that work with registering and combating threats against Russia's information society. But this is not considered to be sufficient since information technology is interconnected in global networks. This means that a threatening actor can operate from anywhere in the world, which makes it difficult to identify the threat and to decide its purpose. Moreover, the number of persons with sufficient computer knowledge in order to disseminate viruses and that can carry out hostile attacks against the IT infrastructure is rapidly increasing. In order to better control threats outside its borders, the Russian governmental power aims at collaborating with partners in other states and international organisations. Several examples of this exist. During 2004, the Russian IT minister[86] invited an Indian delegation to discuss possible cooperations within the IT sphere. This led to an Indian Computer Emergency Response Team (CERT) planning cooperation with Russia in order to combat cyber crime by improving security to prevent cyber attacks.[87]

Also in 2007 experts on information security, policemen, and business representatives from Russia and France participated in a conference in Moscow devoted to the struggle with cyber crime. As a result they have agreed upon about joint efforts and have noted that the problem with phishing has a

---

[86] At that point in time it was Leonid Reiman.
[87] "India to work jointly with Russia to tackle cyber crime".

unilateral character: requisites of the Russian users are not necessary to the French hackers.[88]

Russia is therefore engaged with international organisations in order to develop international treaties and laws. Russian officials have on several occasions proposed that the international community take additional measures to counter cyber-terrorist threats because they fear that terrorists will exploit the Internet's global reach to circumvent these domestic protections. At the time of the July 2006 Group-8 summit in St. Petersburg, for instance, the chairman of the Russian State Duma described the existing legal basis for countering increasingly sophisticated cyber-terrorism threats as inadequate.[89]

On June 7, 2006, acting Foreign Minister Sergei Lavrov stated that the Russian government wanted to work through the United Nations to achieve universal legislation against terrorist threats, adding that Russian officials believe that in some cases regional organizations could prove more flexible and innovative. Lavrov cited the Commonwealth of Independent States (CIS), the Collective Security Treaty Organization (CSTO), and the Shanghai Cooperation Organization (SCO) as particularly important given their "geographic and political proximity" to Russia. CSTO

---

[88] "Rossiya i Franciya ob``edinyatsya v bor`be s xakerami i fisherami".
[89] "Citing Cyber-Terrorism Threat, Russia Explores Internet Controls". Moreover Group-8 consists of Canada, France, Germany, Italy, Japan, Russia, the United Kingdom and the United States. The ministerial meetings bring together ministers responsible for various portfolios to discuss issues of mutual or global concern. The range of topics include health, law enforcement, labour, economic, and social development, energy, environment, foreign affairs, justice and interior, terrorism, and trade.

members include Russia and six former Soviet Republics and the SCO is made up of Russia, China, and four former Soviet republics.[90]

At their June 2006 summit, the leaders of the SCO governments issued a joint declaration on "international information security." The statement expressed concern that modern information and communication technologies represented a danger "for the entire world tantamount to that from the use of weapons of mass destruction." The declaration also warned that the new technologies could interfere "in the internal affairs of sovereign states" and "for criminal, terrorist, military, and political purposes that . . . [will] trigger social instability in countries." They also announced the formation of an expert group to develop detailed recommendations for managing the issue. This working group developed a set of measures for consideration by SCO governments in 2007.[91]

Since a hostile actor can operate from anywhere in the world, Russia is seeking international cooperation. To combat these threats the Russian state is engaged in bilateral cooperation with other states. Moreover, both global international organisations, such as the UN, and regional international organisations, such as CIS and SCO, have been used to develop international treaties and laws. That the Russian governmental power seeks international cooperation shows that these threat images have the character of a "global threat image".

---

[90] "Citing Cyber-Terrorism Threat, Russia Explores Internet Controls".
[91] "Citing Cyber-Terrorism Threat, Russia Explores Internet Controls".

3.5. What is threatened?

In security concepts and the information security doctrine it is emphasized that threats against Russia's information society often are linked to vulnerabilities in the IT infrastructure. Construction flaws increase the vulnerability and give intruders like cyber criminals an increased likelihood of finding information in communication networks and software applications. Another factor is that information and telecommunication networks have become increasingly interconnected across national borders, which causes a dependency on the security of other states' networks.[92]

There are intentional and unintentional threats against Russia's information society. Unintentional disturbances in the communication networks can arise because the required specifications for those components used in the communication networks are insufficient. This can cause functional flaws.[93] Moreover, by mistake researchers and engineers can develop insufficient security programmes to the communication networks.[94] Intentional disturbances can be hackers trying to affect and manipulate the communication networks' control centrals, routers, etc.[95]

Besides the threats and vulnerabilities that can influence the whole of Russian information society, the information

---

[92] "Kontseptciya informacionnoj bezopasnosti setej svyazi obshhego pol`zovaniya vzaimouvyazannoj setej svyazi Rossiskoj Federacii", p. 9-11.
[93] "Ibid".
[94] "Kontseptciya informacionnoj bezopasnosti setej svyazi obshhego pol`zovaniya vzaimouvyazannoj setej svyazi Rossiskoj Federacii", p. 13-14.
[95] "Kontseptciya informacionnoj bezopasnosti setej svyazi obshhego pol`zovaniya vzaimouvyazannoj setej svyazi Rossiskoj Federacii", p. 13-15.

security doctrine also emphasized that threats against different public interests should be noted. These are the economic sector, the internal and external political sphere, the scientific and the technical sphere, the spiritual sphere, the defence sector, the judicial system and information and telecommunication systems.[96]

3.6. The economic sector

With Russia's transition to a market economy, the business community has increased its importance in Russian society. Today Russia's economic sector is dependent on IT systems that collect, process, transfer information of finances, and exchange currencies, taxes, and customs. If these IT systems have insufficient protection, the systems might malfunction, which could lead to important information disappearing. An insufficient protection of the IT systems also means that criminals get an opportunity to hack computer systems and networks at banks and short-term credit institutions in order to get access to information.[97]

---

[96] "Doktrina informacionnoj bezapasnosti Rossiskoj Federacii", p. 5-7. Even if my aim is not to study all mentioned aspects of Russia's perception of information security in each sector/sphere, I have chosen to summarize a survey of different threat images in each sector/sphere. This survey is Appendix 2. For a complete description, see "Doktrina informacionnoj bezapasnosti Rossiskoj Federacii." In the current text I give examples on threat images against the economic sector, the national information and communication systems and the defence sphere.

[97] "Doktrina informacionnoj bezapasnosti Rossiskoj Federacii", p. 13.

3.7. The national information and telecommunication systems

As expected, threats against and vulnerabilities in Russia's national information and telecommunication systems are framed as an information security problem. This concerns actor threat as well as non-actor. Actor threats include foreign intelligence services, organized crime, and individuals trying to access information in national IT systems. This vulnerability increases also when the personnel managing the information and telecommunication systems do not follow the prescribed regulations for collecting, processing, storing, and transferring information. Non-actor threats can be construction flaws in hardware and software crashes in information and telecommunication systems. A reason for these errors can be that uncertified products and systems are used in important IT-systems in society.[98]

3.8. The defence sector

Also threats against and problems with IT systems within the defence sector are considered to be a threat against Russia's national security. This is divided into external and internal threats. External threats against the information security are intelligence activity targeted against Russia's society and Russia's defence interests, for instance, intelligence services carrying out sabotage via information psychological operations.[99] Internal threats against

---

[98] "Doktrina informacionnoj bezapasnosti Rossiskoj Federacii", p. 19.
[99] "Doktrina informacionnoj bezapasnosti Rossiskoj Federacii", p. 21-22.

the defence's information security can be personnel in the Ministry of Defence institutions and within the defence industry that are not following the prescribed procedures for collecting, processing, storing, and transferring information.[100] This can cause IT systems to malfunction or make it easier for intruders to get access to information.

3.9. Dominant threat images

The existence of threats against Russia's information society has been accepted on the Russian political security agenda. But is the perception of threats against information society equal with the existing concrete threats? If one compares the political elite's framing of threat images with the concrete threats against an information society, it raises a couple of interesting questions and answers. Has the Russian governmental power emphasized some threats against its information society more than others? The answer becomes evident by using the matrix that presents concrete IT threats, actor based digital and physical threats, and non-actors based threats, which are construction flaws and natural disasters.

3.10. Digital actor threats

The information security doctrine emphasize that it is important for the governmental power to face threats caused by information warfare and to counteract cyber crime.[101]

---

[100] "Doktrina informacionnoj bezapasnosti Rossiskoj Federacii", p. 24.
[101] "Doktrina informacionnoj bezapasnosti Rossiskoj Federacii", p. 27.

The dissemination of information technology in society has not only created advantages but also led to new types of vulnerabilities, such as cyber crime. IT is misused for criminal acts like accessing confidential information, stealing money, and tax fraud. Hackers may target these attacks against banks' and short-term credit institutions' computer systems and communication networks. In progress with Russia's development towards an information society, IT crime has increased considerably, which is evident in the table beneath.

Table 1. Numbers of registered Cyber crimes[102]

	1998	1999	2002	2003	2004	2005	2006
Source A	71	852					
Source B			4049	7540	8739		
Source C						10214	
Source D							8889

During 1999 the police registered 852 cases of cyber crime in Russia, a twelve-fold increase from the year before.[103] For the year 2004 the statistics show 8739 registered cases, which is an increase of 15,9 percent from previous year.[104] In 2003 the number of registered cyber crime cases was 7540 cases, which is an 86,2

---

[102] It has not been possible to find any statistics on cyber crime for 2000 and 2001. Source A is not a public source, while source B that represents 2002, 2003, and 2004, is found on the web page of the Ministry of Interior, which does not have any online sources dated before 2002. Source A are "Hacker took over control of a Russian gas SCADA system?"; "Interv`yu Pervogo Zamestitelya Sekretarya Soveta bezopasnosti Rossiskoj Federatcii V.P. Sherstyuka gazete "Krasnaya Zvezda", Opublikovannoe 24 Yanvarya 2001 goda", p. 5-6. Source B is "Sostoyanie prestupnosti v Rossiskoj Federatcii za yanvar` - dekabr` 2004 goda", p. 5. Source C is "Obsjtie svedeniya o sostoyanii prestupnosti – 2005", p. 5. Source D is "Obsjtie svedeniya o sostoyanii prestupnosti – 2006", p. 13.
[103] "Hacker took over control of a Russian gas SCADA system?".

percent increase from previous year.[105] By converting percent to numbers you have 4049 cases year 2002. Although it has not been possible to find statistics for all years, the tendency is clear: the more Russia's society becomes digitalised, the more computer crime increases. In 2006 there is a decrease in cases, but it still remains to be seen if the trend is broken.

Technical schools produce tens of thousands of exceptional technical minds that enter a job market with prospects almost universally below their abilities, leading many into the criminal underground, including cyber crime.[106] The Russian cyber police, Department K, tries to restrain this crime. Dmitri Chepchugov the chief of Department K, is of the opinion that IT criminals can be divided into three groups:

"First, the most numerous one includes "cool hackers": children and teenagers who saw something, tried and do it to satisfy their curiosity. They steal passwords of Internet access, break protection of computer programs, and change the contents of web sites. People with broken mentality, unsatisfied with their status and those who did not find their life place belong to the second group. When improving their hacking skills they affirm themselves in the virtual world and are capable of performing the most unpredictable actions. The third group consists of professional criminals. They are easy to deal with. They clearly realized what risk they would run and that is why they will completely get out of a difficulty."[107]

---

[104] "Sostoyanie prestupnosti v Rossiskoj Federatcii za yanvar` - dekabr` 2004 goda", p. 5.

[105] "Sostoyanie prestupnosti v Rossiskoj Federatcii za yanvar` - dekabr` 2003 goda", p. 5.

[106] "The VeriSign Security Review—September 2007".

[107] "Chief of "K" department is interviewed on cyber-crimes".

However, foreign companies have experienced that the Russian police are largely apathetic towards cyber crime, which is not considered a worthwhile use of officers' time, especially when cyber criminals' main victims are foreign entities. However, when a cyber criminal acts upon important domestic companies or government assets, the invasive powers of the Russian police are often brought to bear swiftly and forcefully. With fewer legal checks on their investigative strategies, Russian police can often get fast results.[108]

Digital threats do not necessarily mean cyber criminals, however; they can also refer to international terrorist organisations that hack themselves into IT systems and networks in order to get access to information in private companies or authorities. Also hostile states can hack themselves into networks in order to carry out information psychological operations[109] by disseminating material on Internet.[110] In Russia, psychotronic weapons are perceived as a way of carrying out information psychological operations. According to Russian perceptions, psychotronic weapons[111] are developed everywhere in the world. It would be particularly dangerous if these ended up in the hands of states that support terrorist groups or criminal groups. Psychotronic

---

[108] "The VeriSign Security Review – September 2007".

[109] "Doktrina informacionnoj bezapasnosti Rossiskoj Federacii", p. 7,9 and 14; "Interv`yu Pervogo Zamestitelya Sekretarya Soveta bezopasnosti Rossiskoj Federatcii V.P. Sherstyuka gazete "Krasnaya Zvezda", Opublikovannoe 24 Yanvarya 2001 goda", p. 3.

[110] Polikanov, D. 2001, p. 20.

[111] According to the researcher Viktor Solntsev at the anti-psychotronic centre in Moscow psychotronic weapons is used to affect information in the human mind.

weapons are used against the people's psyche in order to cause hallucinations, sickness and disease, complete apathy, or even death. According to Russian researchers within this working field, radiation from some energy information fields can cause diseases, disturb the function of internal body organs, cause behavioural changes, paralyse the ability to think, and destroy personality, etc.[112]

Russia is (in)famous for its hackers that operate as well nationally as internationally. The first well-known public case of cyber crime in Russia was in 1991 when 125.500 American dollars were stolen by Russian hackers from the soviet bank Vnesheconombank. However, they were caught and sentenced by the Russian judicial system.[113]

Another known Russian case was when hackers attacked Gazprom in 1999. Gazprom is the world's largest producer of natural gas to West Europe, and Russia's largest company; the government owns a significant amount of the shares. The Ministry of Interior's directorate for control of high-technological crime reported an attempt to hack into Gazprom's IT systems. By using an insider the hackers bypassed Gazprom's security systems and broke into the systems that controlled the gas

---

[112] Saarelainen, J. 1999, p. 60–61. "Interv`yu Pervogo Zamestitelya Sekretarya Soveta bezopasnosti Rossiskoj Federatcii V.P. Sherstyuka gazete "Krasnaya Zvezda," Opublikovannoe 24 Yanvarya 2001 goda", p. 7.

[113] Saytarly, T. Examples on laws that are applicable on cyber crime in Russia is article 272—"Illegal access to computer information", article 273—"Creation, the use and distribution of the malicious codes" and article 274—"Infringement with work of computers, systems and networks."

flow in pipelines. The perpetrators were caught and sentenced in court.[114]

Most cyber crime is of the same kind as before, but the tool is new. Other IT crime is a product of the information age. An example on this was when two persons from Rostov-na-Donu were arrested in October 1999 because they sold CD-ROMs containing computer viruses. The virus was not hidden in another programme; rather, the virus itself was the product. The accused confessed that they understood the dangers with disseminating viruses, but they also acknowledged that a demand for these viruses existed. They were indicted and sentenced according to article 273 in The Criminal Code of Russia that forbids creative use or dissemination of dangerous computer programs.[115]

The Russian governmental power considers it problematic when international groups launch cyber attacks against Russia's information society. Russian authorities have found signs that radical fundamentalists have shown interests in using computers as weapons. Among other things they point out that the English imam Abu Hamza al-Masri[116] has collected group computer specialists around himself, which is considered to be indirect evidence that extreme Muslim groups have understood the potential of cyber terrorism.[117]

---

[114] "Hackers cracked Gazprom security, controlled gas-flow switchboard".
[115] "Information Technology and Legislation in Russia".
[116] He is also known as Mustafa Kemal.
[117] "Cracks in the System".

In the information security doctrine, threats against the internal political sphere are framed as a serious concern. An example of this was during the parliamentary poll in December 2007, when politicians discovered websites like YouTube and cyber crime started to become a big issue in political campaigns. Some Russians fear that hacking into oppositional parties' sites has become the latest electioneering weapon. In Russian cyberspace, a political battle is being waged. Political analyst Stanislav Belkovsky has no doubt the Kremlin wants to control the Internet by fair means or foul. He says:

> "I believe that some pro-Kremlin groups, created and financed by Kremlin, are behind those attacks, and I'm quite sure the Kremlin is pure interested in getting the efficient control over the internet sphere."[118]

It is obvious that digital actor threats are considered problematic for Russia's information society and for the interests of the Russian governmental power. Much of the concern regards cyber crime, but cyber terrorism is also framed as a threat. Even if oppositional political campaigns on the Internet are not officially framed as threats, most probably the government has an interest in monitoring and controlling this communication forum.

---

[118] "PM—Political cyber crime rife in Russia".

3.11. Physical actor threats

To review, physical actor threats constitute intentional or unintentional extraneous impact on the infrastructure. Unintentional threats can be the human factor such as negligence or poor security procedures, which might increase incidents. An intentional threat can be someone with explosives or a sledgehammer that sabotage the infrastructure.

Introducing international IT security standards from the International Standardization Organisation (ISO) is a way to increase the awareness about which security procedures that is necessary in society. An example on such a security standard is ISO/IEC 17799 Information Technology—Code of Practice for Information Security Management. This standard is considered important for companies and authorities, since it points out that most security incidents derive from non-technical factors like inadequate organisation and/or because of employee mistakes. The Russian Bureau for Standardisation has adopted the standard[119], as well as the ISO 27002 that recently superseded the more familiar ISO 17799 and ISO 17799:2005 Codes of Practice.[120] The new IT standard is a development of the others and addresses the same issues.[121]

Examples do exist of intentional attacks that have destroyed infrastructure IT is dependent upon. At the end of May 2005, southern Moscow and two nearby regions were hit by an

---

[119] "ISO 17799 News".
[120] "ISO/IEC 27002".
[121] "The VeriSign Security Review—September 2007".

extensive power outage. The power outage depended on a fire caused by an explosion at a subway station in Moscow. A spokesperson for the energy company RAO UES believed it could be sabotage. According to the Minister for Energy[122], the explosion resulted in several transformers being destroyed. The disruption stopped the stock exchange and disturbed hospital equipment and the mobile phone network. It also meant that computers and IT systems malfunctioned.[123]

However, neither in the information security doctrine nor in the concept for information security in Russia's communication networks or among politicians does one find physical actor threats to be emphasized. What can be found is that the Russian Standardisation Bureau has adopted IT standards in order to address some physical actor threats. Still, the conclusion must be that on the political security agenda, this threat image has not gained as much attention as digital threats.

3.12. Construction flaws

Construction flaws arise when IT systems have an insufficient security level or an insufficient operating method. IT systems that are not sufficiently dimensioned can be a threat, since this can cause an overload of the systems whereupon among other thing switchboards and routers collapse. The flaws can be malfunctions

---

[122] At that point in time it was Viktor Khristenko.
[123] "Putin Blames UES Power Monopoly for Moscow Outage"; "Russian Officials Say Power Cut Caused by Fire, Sabotage Not Ruled Out"; "Southern Moscow Hit by Power Outage".

(bugs) in IT systems, which can cause threats against societies. This problem has been noticed in different policy documents, such as the information security doctrine, where it is established that malfunctions in hardware and crashes in software used in information and telecommunication systems can become a threat to society. The existence of malfunctions in hardware and software depend on various factors, for example, the use of uncertified information and telecommunication products. The reasons for using uncertified IT products often depend on these being cheaper than certified. There is also a concern that companies without a governmental licence to produce and develop information and telecommunication systems are involved in this work.[124] The problem concerns the difficulty in verifying and guaranteeing that these products have a sufficient security level.

Chereskin and Tsygichko state that vulnerabilities and malfunctions in software are a general problem for Russia's society. The reason is that substandard software increases the risk of information changing or disappearing in IT systems. Moreover, they mean that Microsoft's operating systems can have embedded trojans that later on can be used by hostile actors.[125]

One of the better-known cases of a construction flaw is the Y2K-bug.[126] In Russia, the Y2K-bug was framed as a technical problem based on the idea that advanced IT systems

---

[124] "Doktrina informacionnoj bezapasnosti Rossiskoj Federacii", p. 6, 9, and 19.
[125] Chereskin, D. and Tsygichko, V, 2005.
[126] The description of the Y2K-bug case is a shortened presentation of a study made by Holmgren and Softa, 2001; Holmgren and Softa, 2002.

could not handle years correctly after the millennium shift. The results could vary from simple miscalculations to total shutdowns of systems. The malfunctions would depend on a computer program, used by the computer industry, where it was common to use two numbers in order to present years instead for four.[127] Also, so-called embedded systems had to a large extent used the same date system, and the problems incredible reach depended on the fact that in most societies there were computer chips in different products and systems with electronic components—for instance, in aeroplanes, elevators and industrial equipment. However, representatives from the Russian government[128] toned down this threat image because Russia in comparison with many states in general had been less exposed to extensive problems, which depended on the factors presented beneath:

1. The Russian government had preferred other programme languages than COBOL, which was common in the West. COBOL is an older programme language that was considered particularly sensitive for the millennium shift problem.[129]

2. The Russian personal computer market was relatively young and therefore there were more computers that were less vulnerable to the Y2K-bug.

---

[127] "Obrashenie"; "Tipovoe polozhenie"; "Metodicheskie rekomendacii po resheniyu "Problemy 2000"", p. 1.
[128] Among others, Sergey Rogov (who was an adviser to the Russian Dumas unit for foreign policy, adviser to the Board for the Ministry of Foreign Affairs, and member of the advising board for the Russian Security Council).
[129] "Russia and Y2K Risks".

3. Russia was less computerized than many countries, for instance, the U.S.

4. In Russia, pirate duplication of upgrading programs was common and contributed to the fact that many computers often could be upgraded because these programmes were cheap.[130]

In Russia, a national action plan was implemented to handle the Y2K problem and a clear division of responsibility, which meant that each agency with a responsibility for a certain activity also was responsible for that 2000 adaptation.[131] In Russia, the Y2K-bug was considered a relatively simple technical problem but rather time-consuming to solve, due to the fact that not only traditional information systems and personal computers were vulnerable problems at the millennium shift. Even more problematic was that no one could assess what would happen at the millennium shift. Therefore, the 2000 problem was *also* framed as a problem with societal consequences for all sectors and people. Because of the uncertainty surrounding the 2000 problem, different threat images were discussed in Russia, for instance, that computer-controlled infrastructure in the energy, finance, transport, and telecommunication sectors could be affected by the millennium

---

[130] "Y2K A Global Ticking Bomb?"; "Ryssarna fruktar inga Y2K-problem".
[131] "Nacional`ny´j plan dejstvij po resheniyu "Problemy 2000" v Rossijskoj Federatcii", p. 2.

bug. Also more ordinary things with embedded microchips could be affected, such as elevators.[132]

After the millennium bug there have been many construction flaws in software and hardware. In mid-November 2007, a construction flaw was found in all versions of Windows XP and Windows 2003, which gave hackers access to personal computer and allowed them to steal passwords and send out spam.[133] However, this construction flaw and others have not had the same impact on the political security agenda as the Y2K-bug.

When the Y2K-bug was on the agenda, the Russian governmental powers attention to construction flaws was biggest, but also after the millennium shift there was awareness that construction flaws in IT could cause problems for critical functions in society like the energy and finance sectors.

3.13. Natural disasters

Natural disasters that are a threat against the IT infrastructure are, for example, storms, earthquakes, flooding, and avalanches, since these can cause interruptions in the power supply and the telecommunication networks. It is necessary that these infrastructures function in order for Internet, e-mail, etc, to function.

According to my findings, I have not in any policy document or in any statement by politicians discovered that natural

---

[132] "Plan Meropriyatij"; "Nacional`ny´j plan dejstvij po resheniyu "Problemy 2000" v Rossijskoj Federatcii", p. 2; "Problema 2000".
[133] "Microsoft Windows: a new flaw".

disasters are framed as a threat against Russia's information society. Still, there exist examples of natural disasters disturbing or causing interruptions in the power supply and telecommunications. Such an example is the earthquake in the Sakhalin region in 1995, when the city Neftegorsk was hit. EMERCOM was brought in with their knowledge about how natural disasters can affect the Russian population and disrupt important societal functions. In Neftegorsk the earthquake reached 7,6 on the Richter scale, but since Neftegorsk is located on the sparsely populated Kamchatka peninsula, less people were affected than during equally strong earthquakes on other locations. Also, the economic losses were less extensive. Despite this, almost 2000 persons were killed immediately, approximately 400 were injured, and 400 were reported missing; in relative terms the city lost 72 percent of its population.[134] The region is rich in oil and gas deposits and as a result has a developed infrastructure with pipelines and electricity grids, etc. When the earthquake hit Neftegorsk, the power network stopped functioning and communication lines were broken, making it impossible to contact the surrounding world.[135] Two hundred kilometres power networks and 300-kilometre telecommunication networks were destroyed[136] and interruptions in these infrastructures led to malfunctioning IT.

---

[134] Porfiriev and Svedin, p. 131. 141.
[135] Porfiriev and Svedin, p. 143.
[136] Porfiriev and Svedin, p. 168.

Despite this and other concrete examples of natural disasters disturbing the function of Russia's information society, they have not been framed as threats on the political agenda.

4. Final discussion

I have examined which threats the Russian governmental power thinks there are against its information society, if the threats have changed over time, and if this is a prioritised question. I also identify which authorities have been and are currently working with these issues and whether Russia participates in international cooperations in order to combat threats against its information society. Finally, I have examined how the Russian political elite view threats against its information society, and compares how that perception differs from real existing threats.

In accordance with Russia's increased aspirations to become a developed information society, threats against this have gained salience on Russian political security agenda. In policy documents, such as the national security concepts from 1997 and 2000, IT threats are framed as one among several other threats against society. But with the creation of the information security doctrine, IT threats gained even more importance on the agenda. Moreover, the focus was not only on digital threats; it also included how construction flaws could cause malfunctions in computer programs and that human errors (physical actor threats) could be a factor to malfunctioning IT.

Nowadays, one finds national policy documents with concrete action plans defining which threats should be noticed and how to reduce vulnerabilities in IT infrastructure. Moreover, there are approved international IT security standards in order to increase the general level of IT security in society. Besides this, Russian authorities, as the former FAPSI, have combated threats against Russia's information society before the subject appeared in any information security doctrine. Governmental authorities have had opportunities to influence what IT threats should be emphasized in different security concepts and in the information security doctrine. Nowadays, FSB, FSO and SVR have taken on FAPSI: s responsibilities.

In the childhood of IT development, there was little interest in this technology in the former Soviet Union; but nowadays the Russian governmental power considers development towards an information society to be of the utmost importance. This ambition has also meant that information security has become a prioritised question on the political agenda. The ratification of the information security doctrine and of the concept of information security in Russia's communication networks is an indicator of this. Moreover, there is now the interdepartmental commission for information security in the Security Council. Furthermore, an increasing number of representatives with the Russian governmental power consider that threats against its information society are a question of highest priority.

Several different state bodies, ministries, and authorities are involved in the work of combating various threats against the emerging Russian information society. Some of these, such as the interdepartmental commission for information security, have an advisory function, while others like FSO and Department K work operationally with signal surveillance and fighting cyber criminals. Committee 22 at Russia's Bureau for Standardisation works with preventive measures. By introducing international IT security standards, it wants to reduce vulnerabilities in software and contribute to a better management of IT. There is an increased ambition to find international cooperations since a hacker can operate from anywhere in the whole world.

Threats and vulnerabilities are considered to influence Russia's *entire* information society as well as threats that are *specific* to different societal sectors. The factors that constitute threats against the entire Russian information society are often linked to vulnerabilities in IT infrastructure. They can be unintentional or intentional disturbances of the communication networks. An unintentional disturbance can be due to flaws in components that are used in communication networks, which turn can lead to these not functioning adequately. Intentional disturbances can depend on hackers trying to influence and manipulate communication networks' control centrals, switches, routers, etc. Another vulnerability, is due to the fact that information and telecommunication networks have become increasingly interconnected across national borders, making it difficult for Russia to guarantee and maintain the security in their own communication networks. Threats against IT are also considered to be *specific* to the economic sector, the internal and external political sphere, the scientific and the technical sphere, the spiritual sphere, the defence sector, the judicial system, and information and telecommunication systems.

Within both the political elite and policy documents one finds that digital threats have gained a lot of attention. In policy documents, as in the information security doctrine, emphasis is on the importance of government in facing threats from information warfare and counteracting cyber crime. The director for Russia's cyber police means that the dissemination of computer technology in society has not only created advantages but also created new ways of carrying out crime, namely via cyber crime. Moreover, Imam Mustafa Kemal has collected group computer specialists around himself, which Russian authorities interpret as an interest in developing cyber terrorism.

Neither in the information security doctrine nor in any security concept has physical actor threat been emphasized as a threat against Russia's information society. Nor do any political statements exist that emphasize physical actor threats as threats against Russia's information society. This implies that physical threats have not gained equal salience on the agenda as digital threats.

Russian authorities, such as the technical committee for information technology, have awareness about the problems construction flaws in IT can cause concerning vital societal functions as the energy, telecommunication, and finance sectors. However, with politicians the awareness of construction flaws was most prominent before the millennium shift, when the Y2K-bug was on the agenda.

An example of a natural disaster that disrupted the power supply and the IT communication was when the earthquake hit Neftegorsk 1995. It not only took 2000 lives but also destroyed 300 kilometres of communication network. Despite the occurrence of natural disasters, it has not been framed as a threat against Russia's information society, neither in any policy document nor in any statements of politicians.

By ranking the four different types of threat images, digital actor threats, physical actor threats, construction flaws, and natural disasters it is possible to find out which ones that have had and currently are having most attention on the agenda.

1. Digital actor threats
2. Construction flaws
3. Physical actor threats
4. Natural disasters

As mentioned, digital threats and construction flaws have gained most attention on the Russian political security agenda. The reason might be that lasting disturbances and extensive interruptions in IT systems can have large consequences on society. The economic losses can be high if critical societal sectors as the energy and finance sector are affected. But should not also physical actor threats and natural disasters gain more attention on the political security agenda as threats against Russia's information society?

Whatever reason for a disruption in the IT, when it is disrupted an information society will not function properly. If politicians and decision-makers do not notice different types of threats against the information society, insufficient risk management of vital functions in society could be the result. Therefore, it is important for the Russian governmental power, and also for other states, to not only emphasizes digital threats and construction flaws.

References

Alberts, D. & Papp, D. (red.) (1997). *The Information Age: An Anthology on Its Impacts and Consequences*. Vol. 1, part 3: *Government and the Military*. Washington DC: National Defense University.

Alberts, D. S. (1996) *Defensive Information Warfare*, Washington: National Defense University.

Beck, Ulrich, (1999) *World Risk Society*. London: Polity.

Buzan, B., Waever, O. and Jaap de Wilde, (1998) *Security: A New Framework for Analysis*. Boulder: Lynne Rienner Publishers, Inc.

Chereskin, D. and Tsygichko, V., Interview at ISA 2005-05-17.

Chereskin, D. (red.) *Problemi Upravleniya Informatsionnoj Bezopasnostyu,* 2002. Moscow: ISA RAN.

"Chief of "K" department is interviewed on cyber-crimes". Retrieved 2005-02-28 from http://www.crime-research.org/news/2003/05/Mess1202.html

"Citing Cyber-Terrorism Threat, Russia Explores Internet Controls". Retrieved 2008-01-10 from http://www.hudson.org/index.cfm?fuseaction=publication_details&id=5205

"Cracks in the System". Retrieved 2003-02-12 from
http://www.time.com/time/europe/magazine/article/0,13005,901
020617-260664,00.html

Denning, D. (1999) *Information Warfare and Security*. Reading,
Mass.: ACM Press Books.

"Doktrina informacionnoj bezapasnosti Rossiskoj Federacii".
Retrieved 2008-01-03 from
http://www.scrf.gov.ru/documents/5.html

"E´kologicheskaya doktrina Rossiskoj Federacii. (2002)".
Retrieved 2004-07-11 from
http://www.scrf.gov.ru/documents/24.html

"E-Moscow – a $2 Billion Program". Retrieved 2007-12-01 from
http://www.centerdigitalgov.com/international/story.php?
docid=61324

Entman, R. (1993) "Framing: Toward Clarification of a Fractured
Paradigm" in *Journal of Communication* 43 (4).

Eriksson, J. (2004) *Kampen om hotbilden—Rutin and drama i
svensk säkerhetspolitik*. Stockholm: Santérus Förlag.

Eriksson, J. (ed.) (2001). *Hotbildernas politik*. Stockholm:
Utrikespolitiska institutet.

"e-russia." (2001). Retrieved 2005-02-01 from http://www.e-
russia.ru/program

"FAPSI". Retrieved 2007-09-03 from
http://en.wikipedia.org/wiki/FAPSI

"FAPSI Operations". Retrieved 2003-02-12 from
http://www.fas.org/irp/world/russia/fapsi/ops.htm

"FAPSI—The Federal Agency of Government Communications and Information". Retrieved 2005-01-24 from http://www.agentura.ru/english/dosie/brit/fapsi

"Federal Agency for Government Communications and Information". Retrieved 2003-02-17 from http://www.globalsecurity.org/intell/world/russia/fapsi.htm

"Federal`naya sluzhba bezopasnosti Rossii (FSB)". Retrieved 2005-08-12 from http://www.agentura.ru/dossier/russia/fsb

"Foreign Intelligence Service (Russia)". Retrieved 2007-11-22 from http://en.wikipedia.org/wiki/Foreign_Intelligence_Service_(Russia)

"The Foreign Policy Concept of the Russian Federation". http://www.fas.org/nuke/guide/russia/doctrine/econcept.htm

"FSB Looks An Awful Lot Like The KGB". Retrieved 2005-05-16 from http://www.chechentimes.org/en/comments/?id=9918

"GRU". Retrieved 2007-11-23 from http://en.wikipedia.org/wiki/GRU

"Hackers cracked Gazprom security, controlled gas-flow switchboard". Retrieved 2005-05-16 from http://www.asmconsortium.com/asm/asm_imps.nsf/0/07256aed005eb4ca862568e300672ced?OpenDocument

"Hacker took over control of a Russian gas SCADA system?". Retrieved 2005-05-16 from http://lists.iinet.net.au/pipermail/scada/2004-May/000074.html

Hinnfors, J. (1995). *På dagordningen? Svensk politisk stil i förändring*. Stockholm: Nerinuis and Santérus Förlag AB.

Hildreth, S. (2001). *Cyberwarfare*. http://www.fas.org/irp/crs/RL30735.pdf

Holmgren, J. and Softa, J. (2003). *The Functional Security Agenda of the Nordic States*. Stockholm: The Swedish Institute of International Affairs.

Holmgren, J. & Softa, J. (2002). *Millenniebuggen på dagordningen —en komparativ analys av 2000-frågan i Ryssland, Sverige and USA*. Stockholm: The Swedish Emergency Management Agency.

Holmgren, J. & Softa, J. (2001). *Årtusendet hot? Y2k-buggen på dagordningen i Ryssland, Sverige and USA*. Stockholm: The Swedish Institute of International Affairs.

"India to work jointly with Russia to tackle cyber crime". Retrieved 2005-06-08 from http://www.crime-research.org/news/06.12.2004/827

"Information Technology and Legislation in Russia". Retrieved 2005-08-27 from http://www.ku.edu/~herron/info_policy/it_pol_ru.html

"Internet Law—Strategy for Developing an Information Society in Russia". Retrieved 2007-11-22 from http://www.ibls.com/internet_law_news_portal_view.aspx?s=latestnews&id=1862

"Interv`yu Pervogo Zamestitelya Sekretarya Soveta bezopasnosti
Rossiskoj Federatcii V.P. Sherstyuka gazete "Krasnaya
Zvezda," Opublikovannoe 24 Yanvarya 2001 goda". Retrieved
2005-06-23 from http://www.ln.mid.ru/ns-
osndoc.nsf/0/432569fa003a249c432569ed004ce6c8?
OpenDocument

"ISO/IEC 27002". Retrieved 2007-11-22 from
http://www.vniki.ru/document/4169474.aspx

"ISO 17799 News". Retrieved 2005-08-20 from
http://www.molemag.net/

Jervis, R. (1976). *Perception and Misperception in International
Politics.* Princeton: Princeton University Press.

Kingdon, John (1995). *Agendas, Alternatives and Public Choices.*
Second edition. New York: Harper Collins College Publishers.

Kontseptciya informacionnoj bezopasnosti setej svyazi obshhego
pol`zovaniya vzaimouvyazannoj setej svyazi Rossiskoj
Federacii. Moscow: Ministry for Information Technologies and
Telecommunications.

"Kontseptciya naciona`lnoj bezopasnosti Rossiskoj Federacii.
(2000)". Retrieved 2007-06-07 from
http://www.scrf.gov.ru/documents/1.html

Leijonhielm, J. et al. (2000). *Rysk militär förmåga i ett
tioårsperspektiv—en förnyad bedömning 2000.* Stockholm: The
Swedish Defence Research Agency.

Leijonhielm J. et al. (1999). *Rysk militär förmåga i ett tioårsperspektiv.* Stockholm: The Swedish Defence Research Agency.

Malm, A., Softa, J., Andersson, J. J. and K. Lindström. (2003). *IT and sårbarhet – kritiska beroendeförhållanden i den nationella IT-infrastrukturen.* Stockholm: The Swedish Emergency Management Agency.

"Metodicheskie rekomendacii po resheniyu "Problemy 2000."". Retrieved 2008-01-05 from http://www.old.perm.ru/2000/2000.htm

"Mezhvedomstvennyè komissii soveta bezapasnosti Rossiskoj Federacii". Retrieved 2008-01-05 from http://www.scrf.gov.ru/documents/sections/4/

"Microsoft Windows: A New Flaw". Retrieved 2007-11-23 from http://www.crime-research.org/news/18.11.2007/3013

"Ministry of Extraordinary Situations". Retrieved 2005-08-17 from http://en.wikipedia.org/wiki/Ministry_of_Extraordinary_Situations_(Russian_Federation)

"Morskaya doktrina Rossiskoj Federacii na period do 2020 goda. (2001)". Retrieved 2008-01-05 from http://www.scrf.gov.ru/documents/34.html

Mörth, U. (1999) *Framing the Defense Industry/Equipment Issue: The Case of the European Commission.* Stockholm: Score.

"Nacional`ny´j plan dejstvij po resheniyu "Problemy 2000" v Rossijskoj Federatcii". Retrieved 2008-01-05 from http://www.old.perm.ru/2000/mainplan.doc

"National Security Concept of the Russian Federation—1997".
http://www.nupi.no/russland/RIAtext/National_Security_Conce
pt_1997.html

"National Security Concept of the Russian Federation—2000".
http://www.fas.org/nuke/guide/russia/doctrine/gazeta012400.ht
m

"The Network Readiness Index 2006-2007 rankings". Retrieved
2007-11-23 from http://www.weforum.org/pdf/gitr/rankings.pdf

Nicander, L and Ranstorp, M. (2004) *Terrorism in the Information
Age—New Frontiers?* Stockholm: The Swedish National
Defence College.

"Normativnyè akty reglamentiruyushhie deyatel`nost fsb".
Retrieved 2005-03-17 from
http://www.fsb.ru/under/upravlenie.html

Norris, P., Montague, K., and M. Just. (2003) *Framing Terrorism.*
London: Routledge.

"Obsjtie svedeniya o sostoyanii prestupnosti—2006". Retrieved
2007-11-08 from
http://www.mvd.ru/files/oX0.HjeEnTMwA9d.pdf

"Obsjtie svedeniya o sostoyanii prestupnosti—2005". Retrieved
2007-11-08 from http://www.mvd.ru/files/4001.pdf

"Obrashenie". Retrieved 2001-04-04 from
http://www.ptti.gov.ru/gk-doc/2000/obrash.htm

"Otchet FSB za 2003 god". Retrieved 2008-01-05 from
http://www.agentura.ru/Search

"Plan Meropriyatij". Retrieved 2001-04-04 from www.ptti.gov.ru

"PM—Political cyber crime rife in Russia". Retrieved 2007-11-21 from http://www.abc.net.au/pm/content/2007/s2040301.htm

Polikanov, D. (ed.). (2001). *Information Challenges to National and International Security*. Moscow: PIR Center.

Porfiriev, B. et.al. Interview at RIO Center, 2005-05-19.

Porfiriev, B. and Svedin, L. (ed.). (2002). *Crisis Management in Russia—Overcoming Institutional Rigidity and Resources Constraints*. Stockholm: The Swedish Defence Research Agency.

"Problema 2000". Retrieved 2001-04-05 from www.cefey.ru/news/y2k.hm

"Putin Blames UES Power Monopoly for Moscow Outage". Retrieved 2005-08-26 from http://www.mosnews.com/news/2005/05/25/anotherblackout.shtml

"Putin makes sweeping changes to power structures". Retrieved 2005-03-17 from http://www.gazeta.ru/2003/03/11/Putinmakessw.shtml

"Reforma specsluzhb nachalas. Tolko sovsem he tak, kak govoril Putin". Retrieved 2005-03-17 from http://www.agentura.ru/Right?id=20030327230500

Rein, M. and Schön, D. (1993) "Reframing Policy Discourse," in Fischer, F. and Forrester, J (ed.), *The Argumentative Turn in Policy Analysis and Planning*. London: UCL Press Ltd.

"Resursnoe obespechenie programmy". Retrieved 2005-01-07 from http://www.e-russia.ru/program/992960452

"Rostexregulirovanii bydet uchastovat` v vy`borax v Sovet ISO". Retrieved 2005-07-13 from http://www.gost.ru

"Russia and Y2K Risks". Retrieved 2001-04-12 from http://www.aeronautics.ru/russiay2kmain.htm

Russia Approves Draft Information Security Doctrine. Xinhua News Agency.

"Russian and Baltic Economies – the Week in Review 11 # 2003". Retrieved 2005-03-17 from http://www.bof.fi/bofit/eng/3weekly/wpdf/we03.pdf

"Russia—Surveillance of Communications". Retrieved 2005-05-12 from http://www.statewatch.org/news/jun00/rip3.htm

"Russian Officials Say Power Cut Caused by Fire, Sabotage Not Ruled Out". Retrieved 2005-08-26 from http://www.mosnews.com/news/2005/05/25/blackoutreason.shtml

"Rossiya i Franciya ob``edinyatsya v bor`be s xakerami i fisherami". aRetrieved 2007-11-22 from http://www.crime-research.ru/news/03.10.2007/3885

"Ryssarna fruktar inga Y2K-problem". Retrieved 2001-09-24 from http://www.aftonbladet.se/nyheter/9912/27/y2k.html

Saarelainen, Jorma (1999) *Aspekter på ryska Informationskrigföring.* Stockholm: The Swedish National Defence College.

Saytarly, T. *Russia: Computer Crimes Statistics.* Computer Crime Research Center. http://www.crime-research.org/news/13.03.2004/131

SEMA: 0753/2003, 2003. Stockholm: The Swedish Emergency Management Agency.

"SIGINT". Retrieved 2007-11-23 from http://en.wikipedia.org/wiki/SIGINT

"Sluzhba spetsial`noj svyazi i informacii federal`noj sluzhby oxrany`. Rossijskoj Federacii". Retrieved 2005-07-12 from http://www.agentura.ru/dossier/russia/fso/specvyaz

"Sluzhba vneschnej razvedki Rossii". Retrieved 2003-11-12 from http://svr.gov.ru/svr_today/celi.htm

Smoljan, G.L., Tsygichko, V., and Han-Magomedov. (2004). *Internet v Rossii—Perspektivi Razvitiya.* Moscow: ISA RAN.

Softa, Jan (2004) "Framed vs. Real IT Threats—The Case of Estonia," in Callaos, N. et al. (ed.) *The 8th World Multi-Conference on Systemics, Cybernetics and Informatics—July 18-21, 2004.* Orlando: IIIS.

Softa, Jan (2003) *De glömda pusselbitarna i analysen av hot mot IT-samhällets infrastruktur.* Stockholm: The Swedish Institute of International Affairs.

Softa, Jan (2002) *Det ansiktslösa IT-hotet.* The press service of the Swedish Institute of International Affairs. http://www.ui.se/text2002/art3502.htm

"SORM—Russia's big brother". Retrieved 2005-08-16 from http://www.cvni.net/radio/nsnl/nsnl021/nsnl21sorm.html

"Sostav-Mezhvedomstvennoj komissii soveta bezopasnosti rossijskoj federatcii po informacionnoj bezopasnosti po dolzhnostyam". Retrieved 2008-01-05 from http://www.scrf.gov.ru/documents/46.html

"Sostoyanie prestupnosti v Rossiskoj Federatcii za yanvar`-dekabr` 2003 goda". The Ministry of Internal Affairs. http://mvdinform.ru/files/2177.pdf

"Sostoyanie prestupnosti v Rossiskoj Federatcii za yanvar`-dekabr` 2004 goda", The Ministry of Internal Affairs. http://www.mvd.ru/files/3157.pdf

"Southern Moscow Hit by Power Outage". Retrieved 2005-08-26 from http://www.mosnews.com/news/2005/05/25/blackout.shtml

"Sovet bezopasnosti Rossijskoj federatsii—istoriya sozdaniya, pravovoj status, struktura i osnove napravleniya deyatel`nosti". Retrieved 2001-05-03 from http://www.scrf.gov.ru/documents/history.shtml

Space and Electronic Warfare Lexicon: http://www.sew-lexicon.com/gloss_c.htm#CRACKER and http://www.sew-lexicon.com/gloss_h.htm

"Special Communications and Information Service". Retrieved 2007-11-22 from http://www.globalsecurity.org/intell/world/russia/fapsi.htm

"Strategiya razvitiya informacionnogo obshhestva v Rossi". Retrieved 2008-01-11 from http://kremlin.ru/text/docs/2007/07/138695.shtml#

"Tipovoe polozhenie". Retrieved 2001-04-04 from
http://www.ptti.ru.gk-doc/2000/cc_poloz.htm

"TKNo022". Retrieved 2005-07-13 from
http://www.gost.ru/wps/portal/pages.TechCom

Tsygichko, V., (2002). *Geopoliticheskie posledstviya
informatizacii i novy`e vy`zovy` bezopasnosti i Problemy`
upravleniya informacionnoj bezopasnoste.* (ed.) Chersjkin D.
Moscow: URSS.

Tsygichko, V., et. al. (2001). *Informacionnoe Oruzhie i
Mezhdunarodnaya Informacinnaya Bezopasnost.* Moscow: ISA.

Tsymbal, V.I., (1995). "Kontseptsiya 'Informatsionoj Voyny'"
speech given at the Russian-U.S. conference on "Evolving post
Cold War National Security Issues," Moscow 12-14. September
1995.

"Uprazdneny` FSNP i FAPSI, FPS peredana v FSB". Retrieved
2005-03-17 from http://www.agentura.ru/Search

"U.S. & FCS E-Russia Program—Update August 2002". Retrieved
2005-03-01 from
http://www.tiaonline.org/policy/regional/nis/E-russia.pdf

Vendil Pallin, Carolina. The Swedish Defence Research Agency.
E-mail: 2005-05-27.

"The VeriSign Security Review—September 2007". Retrieved
2007-11-21 from
http://www.verisign.com/Resources/Security_Services_Newslett
ers/The_VeriSign_Security_Review/page_042737.html

"Vystuplenie predstavitelya Rossii A.I. Anatonova v Pervom
Komitete 55-j sessii GA OON pri predstavlenii proekta
rezolyucii "Dostizheniya v sfere informatizacii i
telekommunikacii v kontekste mezhdunarodnoj bezopasnosti"
19 oktyabrya 2000 goda". Retrieved 2005-05-26 from
http://www.ln.mid.ru/Ns-
dmo.nsf/arh/432569F10031EB934325699C003C102A?
OpenDocument

"Vliyanie fishinga na razvitie e`lektronnoj kommercii". Retrieved
2007-12- 22 from http://www.crime-
research.ru/analytics/sabodach07

"Voennaya doktrina Rossiskoj Federacii". Retrieved 2005-07-12
from http://www.scrf.gov.ru/documents/33.html

Wiik, W. M. (E-mail) FMV. 2003-06-02.

"Y2K A Global Ticking Bomb?". Retrieved 2001-05-05 from
http://www.csis.org/html/y2k2f.html

"Zadachi Ministerstva". Retrieved 2005-03-22 from
http://www.mchs.gov.ru/print.php?
fid=1054642410756719&cid=1054642410756719

Appendix 1

Acronyms and abbreviations

AIR	Administration of Information Resources
CIS	Commonwealth of Independent States
CERT	Computer Emergency Response Teams
COCOM	Coordinating Committee for Multilateral Export Controls
CSTO	The Collective Security Treaty Organization
Duma	The Russian Parliament
FAPSI	(in English) Federal Agency of Government Communications and Information
FOA	(in English) the former Swedish Defence Research Agency
FOI	(in English) the Swedish Defence Research Agency
FSB	(in English) Federal Security Service
FSO	(in English) Federal Protection Service
FPS	(in English) Federal Border Service
G-8	Group-8

GRU	(in English) Main Intelligence Directorate
HPM-weapon	High Powered Microwave weapon
ICT	Information and Communication Technique
ISA	Institute for System Analysis
ISO	International Standardization Organization
IT	Information Technology
K-department	K does not have any formal meaning but is only a letter
KGB	(in English) Committee for State Security
NATO	North Atlantic Treaty Organization
NRI	Networked Readiness Index
SCO	The Shanghai Cooperation Organization
SEMA	The Swedish Emergency Management Agency
SORM	System of Ensuring Investigative Activity
SVR	(in English) Foreign Intelligence Service
UN	United Nations
Y2K	Year 2000

Appendix 2

The economic sector

With Russia's transformation into a market economy the business community has increased in importance for the function of Russia's society. Nowadays, Russia's business community is depending on IT systems that collect, process, store, and transfer information of finances, exchange currencies, taxes, and more. If these IT systems have insufficient protection, the possibility of malfunction increases, which can cause important information to disappear. An insufficient protection of IT systems also increases the likelihood of criminals hacking into IT systems and networks at banks and credit institutions in order to find information or steal money.[137]

The internal and external political sphere

There is fear that information in Russia and abroad will be misused in order to damage Russia's political interests. This can be through spreading of disinformation about Russia's policy, about the federal authorities' activities, and about events that happen in and outside the country; or to transfer ideas about changing the

---

[137] "Doktrina informacionnoj bezapasnosti Rossiskoj Federacii".

constitutional system and dividing Russia with violence.[138] A threat against the external political sphere is that foreign political, economic, or military groups can carry out information operations in order to influence Russia's foreign policy, or to get access to information in order to influence Russian embassies and bodies abroad.[139] Finally, there is fear that political groups, non-governmental associations, mass media, and individuals by using propaganda will try to influence Russia's foreign policy.[140]

The scientific and technical sphere

The threat image is that industrial states, intelligence services, and private companies will increase industrial espionage against Russia in order to get access to Russian scientific and technical resources, ideas, and inventions that can be used for their own purposes.[141]

The spiritual sphere

A somewhat different information security problem discussed in Russia is threats against the Russian identity/spirit. For some reason, an uncontrolled expansion of foreign media in Russia's information sector is considered one of the more serious threats to the Russian identity. The Russian identity can also be affected if the Russian cultural heritage degenerates. This cultural heritage

---

[138] "Doktrina informacionnoj bezapasnosti Rossiskoj Federacii", p. 16-17.
[139] "Doktrina informacionnoj bezapasnosti Rossiskoj Federacii", p. 17.
[140] "Doktrina informacionnoj bezapasnosti Rossiskoj Federacii", p. 18-19.
[141] "Doktrina informacionnoj bezapasnosti Rossiskoj Federacii", p. 20.

covers archives, museum collections, libraries, and architectural monuments.[142]

The national information and telecommunication systems

As expected, threats against and vulnerabilities in national information and telecommunication systems are framed as a threat against Russia's information security. This includes both actor threats and non-actor. Actor threats are when foreign intelligence services, organized crime groups, and individuals try to get access to information in national IT systems. The vulnerability also increases when the personnel that manage information and telecommunication systems do not follow prescribed procedures for managing of information. Non-actor threats are malfunctions in hardware and crashes in software within information and telecommunication system, which can arise due to use of uncertified products and systems.[143]

The defence sector

Threats against and problems with IT systems within the defence sphere are also framed as threats against Russia's national security. In the information security doctrine both external and internal threats are mentioned. External threats against information security are all types of intelligence activity directed against Russian society and Russian defence interests. This can refer to someone

---

[142] I assume that they discuss these Russian cultural heritages as an information security problem because it gives a sense of decay of the Russian identity/spirit.
[143] "Doktrina informacionnoj bezapasnosti Rossiskoj Federacii", p. 19.

who carries out radio electronic warfare or hacks into computer networks, or to intelligence services carrying out sabotage operations with information psychological operations.[144] Internal threats can be caused by staff in the Ministry of Defence institutions or in the defence industry that do not follow prescribed routines for collecting, processing, storing, and transferring data,[145] causing IT systems malfunction or making it easier for intruders to get access to data.

The judicial system

The threat image consists of other states, international criminal organisations, and private companies trying to get access to security-classified data in the judicial system.[146] Not only are intentional actions framed as a problem, but also errors with the staff that work in the sphere are framed as a threat against the information security. Also malfunctions in hardware and software can cause problems within the judicial system and the law court sphere.[147]

---

[144] "Doktrina informacionnoj bezapasnosti Rossiskoj Federacii", p. 21-22.
[145] "Doktrina informacionnoj bezapasnosti Rossiskoj Federacii", p. 24.
[146] "Doktrina informacionnoj bezapasnosti Rossiskoj Federacii", p. 25.
[147] "Doktrina informacionnoj bezapasnosti Rossiskoj Federacii", p. 24-25.

www.ingramcontent.com/pod-product-compliance
Lightning Source LLC
Chambersburg PA
CBHW051209050326
40689CB00008B/1251